ISLANDS OF EXPERIENCE

ISLANDS OF EXPERIENCE

Poems by
DEAN NICHOLS

Resource *Publications*
An imprint of *Wipf and Stock Publishers*
199 West 8th Avenue • Eugene OR 97401

Resource Publications
A division of Wipf and Stock Publishers
199 W 8th Ave, Suite 3
Eugene, OR 97401

Islands of Experience
By Nichols, Dean
Copyright©1972 by Nichols, Dean
ISBN: 1-59244-875-5
Publication date 9/24/2004
Previously published by Exposition Press, 1972

To Lloyd

Yet all experience is an arch wherethrough
Gleams that untravel'd world whose margin fades
Forever and forever when I move.

ALFRED LORD TENNYSON

I would not ask you to share with me the mainland of my life; for who has half a century to spare? But I invite you to share with me a few of these islands of experience and through them catch a glimpse of an untraveled world.

DEAN NICHOLS

Contents

Acknowledgments	9
Time	13

ALASKA

Painting	15
The Glacier Priest	17
Alaska's Mountains	19
Snowbound	20
Silence	21
Cheechahko's Dream	22
Nature's Song	23
Eklutna	24
Valley of Tomorrow	25
The Mountain's Call	26

ALMA JUNE

Upon Her Face	27
A Silver Song	29
Silver Threads	30
One	31

CONFLICT

Conformity	32
The "News" About My Lai	35

SEARCHING

Landbound Lament	37
The End?	38
Prince William Sound, Alaska	40
A Sailor's Two Loves	41
Our Own	43
Bering River	44
Because I Must	48
Turn Again	49

LLOYD

Why?	51
The Rape of Mind	54
The River	54
My Son's Birthday	57
An Unapprehended Inspiration	57
The Light That Cannot Die	60

BEAUTY AND LOVE

My Cabin Door	62
Love	64
The Manliness of Beauty	65
My Tankard	67
Gray	70
A Splash of Color	72
To a Mother, a Grandmother, and Three Daughters	74
A Glass of Rare Wine	78
The Gift	80

Acknowledgments

To Cimmy, who fanned into flame the spark to publish these lines when he told me, "If someone asks me if I know you, I would of course say yes; but when they ask me who you are, I would, above all else, rather be able to say, 'He is the one who wrote this book.'"

To Alma June, who said, "Why don't you sit down right now and write Exposition Press."

And to those who said with such genuine feeling, "You must write, Dean, just write..."

ISLANDS OF EXPERIENCE

Time

If only I could catch the spinning years
and hold them still—
have nothing change
and no one age
and no Time
chasing at my heels;
for just a day, oh, now and then,
how I would love to catch the years
and hold them still.

I'd fix a rainbow in the sky;
it wouldn't fade,
and wild geese would never fly
beyond the lakes
and perfect lattice-patterned fields.

I'd have one autumn afternoon
filled with summer's ending sun,
and Love
on grassy cushioned glades
with the infinite blue canopy above;
and we would lie in timeless space,
in stillness
far above the Race—

If I could catch the spinning years
and hold them still.

Jo Ann (Nichols) Harris

ALASKA

Painting

You take the brush
and place the oils on canvas there
   and let me play with words.

Paint mountains high, you dare;
but is it really fair
to thrust the brush into my hand?
My medium is words, and rather
with my pen I'd paint the frozen land
and stack the granite crags
into the sky.

Late in the afternoon I'll brush
the shadows deep in those ravines
and glint the softened amber glow
from off the ridges torn
with blowing snow.

And lower down I'll turn
the green trees blue and maybe catch
the sparkle of a waterfall;
or is it ice just standing tall
and waiting for the warmth of spring
to flow again down to the sea?

I took the brush
and daubed the canvas bare
and felt a faint, creative spark,
I must admit;

but would you really care
if here instead on this plain page
I place the symbols man calls words
in such a pattern
that the mountains rise before your eyes,
and laugh once more with sunlight
before they drift into the night and die?

I'll try again;
but really, I believe my pen
is better fitted to my hand.

January 24, 1971

This was my first "Alaskan" poem. My wife had taken up oil painting; we named one of her first real creations, a spectacular, rugged mountain scene:

The Glacier Priest

Across the frigid water stands
the lonely Glacier Priest;
his sermon never ending as
you stand alone and feast
your eyes upon this monument
of God's creation plan
of tall, eternal mountain that
is part of mortal man.

Your ears may strain to listen
to the voice of which I speak
and hear no sound
but the wind around
each tall and lonely peak.
So listen with your eyes my friend,
and think on Him above;
and let the mountain tell your heart
of the vastness of His love.

Climb slowly with your eyes my friend
up ragged center ridge,
and note the care
that was taken there
to carve each stony bridge,
as if in all creation He
had nothing more to do
than to carve this craggy mountain and
create the one called you.

For such is truth,
like eternal mountain,
standing tall and strong:
you were prepared
with far more care
than was this misty song.

So remember, when you leave this place
and reach another shore,
that life is not just food and fun;
this mountain says there's more;
And remember too this Glacier Priest,
when you have gone beyond,
will still be standing there
and preaching
across this arctic pond.

February 23, 1961

And so we fell in love with:

Alaska's Mountains

There are mountains high
and mountains low
and mountains round and worn
and mountains hot and mountains cold
and mountains cragged and shorn
of all but frost and
clinging ice
where the williwaw is born.

Oh give me mountains
for my life,
and give me mountains high,
and give me mountains
streaked with snow
where the lonely eagles fly;

Where life is full,
and life is real,
and it's made for you and I;
where freedom swings
on wild wind wings
and I can live
    with the sun
        and the sky.

February 24, 1961

I named another of my wife's paintings:

Snowbound

Softly, silently, stealthily now,
the soft snow steals away
the freedom of travel the sourdough knew
on the trails of the summer day.

The silent light
of the northern night
takes the place of the summer sun;
but with summer past,
and home at last,
his season's work is done.

Warm in his cabin,
snug in the snow,
it's here
that peace is found.
It's here
that the cares of the world are gone.
Who cares if he is snowbound?

February 25, 1961

Try it sometime; really listen to the silence for a full fifteen minutes. It is difficult to do, but the reward is a startling discovery.

Silence

Beautiful, thrilling, inspiring,
useful and magnificent
as many sounds are,
they are but distortions of the silence.
So until you've really heard the silence,
you have never really listened.
To hear the silence is to hear all sound
in perfect harmony.

I think as I sit in silence
with Alaska all around,
that there's nothing quite so mighty
as the voice of silent sound.

Have you ever really listened when
the earth is soft and still
and heard the roar of silence soar
as no sound ever will?

The sounds of music, voice or song
have beauties oft untold;
but listen to the silent sound,
and hear the truth unfold.

For only when you've heard the sound
of silence, deep, complete,
have you really listened with your heart
and heard your soul's heartbeat.

March 14, 1961

Cheechahko's Dream

You can dream of Alaska's mountains,
and a lake that is icy blue,
and a cabin warm where a northern storm
is a symphony just for you.

You can dream of the call of a waterfall
on a tumbling glacier stream,
and picture there a meadow fair
in your "Cheechahko's Dream."

But you'll not be wrong, you tenderfoot.
Your dream is a vision true;
for Alaska's call is her mountains tall
and her lakes and her glaciers too.

And that silence deep is designed for sleep;
and that cabin's just waiting to grow;
for the timbered land and an eager hand
are the team that can make it so.

So trade your ease for the tundra trees;
leave the world of confusion and strife.
Lift up your eyes to the northern skies,
and discover the secret of life.

June 12, 1961

This vision appeared first in my wife's mind, then on canvas in oils, and only finally on paper in words. It is a lovely thing, isn't it?

Nature's Song

A glacier glows mid mountains tall and cold.
Like the stream that drifts away it's ages old.
Yet year by year the mountain snows press down
to form anew this frozen, jeweled crown.

And out across the tundra from its base
a trapper's cabin nestles in the lace
of trees that formed of waters glacier fed,
and soil ground from rocks that were its bed.

Time is a word, but what is time?
The cabin's old; the trees have stood so long.
Yet in the measure of the river and her crown,
they're both but one refrain from nature's song.

June 13, 1961

Eklutna

By the waters of Eklutna
where the mountains reach the sky,
and Black bear roam the mountainside
and lonely eagles fly,

I find a close communion
with nature's vibrant song
and feel the pulse and depth of life
and know that I belong

Where I can see those mountains high
and walk the Black bear's lair
and hear the wavelets wash the shore
with peaceful, rhythmic care,

And feel the kiss upon my face
the mountain breezes bring.
For when I share Eklutna's home
I hear all nature sing.

July 4, 1961

My wife had painted a skillfully presented, mysterious thing where the depth gave one the distinct feeling that you were peering from a known world into that strange, new, but very real one we vaguely call the future. I named it:

Valley of Tomorrow

Are they mountains? Are they clouds?
Is that a river or a highway?
What does the future really hold
in the "Valley of Tomorrow"?

Can the dreamer really dream?
Can the Prophet really know
what is the way for you or me,
in the "Valley of Tomorrow"?

What does it really matter?
Can you really, really care,
if your way be stream or road,
if the distant clouds are stone,

If as you walk into the valley,
(There's no other way you know),
you hold the child's anticipation
you're so often taught to hold

And see the "Valley of Tomorrow"
as the valley e'er should be:
an invitation to adventure.
Shall we then just wait and see?

August 1, 1961

My beloved son Lloyd and I had taken our boat on a two weeks' hunting trip across Lake Louise, Lake Susitna, Lake Tyone and north down the Tyone River.

Twice we passed the empty village of Tyone, and each time there was much more than just the intense awareness of an abandoned village, there was much, much more. This poem tries to grasp what it was.

The Mountain's Call

Wrapped in the mystery of a people gone
and held in the spell of a spirit,
that is all that is left to tell of their flight,
save a few tumbling cabins
and the empty shell of a crude boat,
I listen for the voice of the past;
and I hear,
faintly but clearly and with a power indescribable
and echoing down the long, cold waters of Lake Tyone,
I hear the mountain's call.

Are they there,
frozen forever in the ageless ice of the mountains,
these people of the Village of Tyone?
Are *they* calling to my searching, questioning mind
from their icy grave
and saying,
"Come, share with us the mountain's bewitching beauty
(and the mountain's terror)
and we will tell you our story."?

Where have they gone,
these people of the Village of Tyone?
Did they,
one day in the measureless past,
fail to resist as I can barely resist
the enveloping magnetism
of the mountain's call?

May 25, 1962

ALMA JUNE

Upon Her Face

I know a woman
across whose years
the ravages of time have written deep and clear,
the story of her life
upon her face.

She's young.
The wrinkles of long years are yet to come, yet
neither will she know again
the carefree days of youth.

But written there in sparkles from her eyes,
and ready laugh,
the gaiety and promise of a child
stand bold and clear.

And motherhood,
that emblem of nobility,
is also written there
in eloquence so rich and pure.

And suffering,
and pain and loss,
and sadness too are found;
and scars of hardwon battles there to see.

But honesty,
that purifying flame of soul,

and will to fight, and victory
show forth
the power of the soul to win its own.

I know a woman,
across whose years,
the ravages of time have written deep and clear,
the story of her life
upon her face.

And as I read,
which daily is my joy,
I read the story of my friend, my sweetheart,
and my wife.
December 16, 1962

To my wife, on our twenty-fifth wedding anniversary

A Silver Song

The silver threads that grace your auburn hair,
the telltale lines fanned out from twinkling eyes,
all sing a song of love and work and care,
a song of silver anniversaries.

Would we, who wish and dream and hope and pray,
call down the gods to wash away those signs?
Would we invoke those powers on this day
to take you back to youth unlearned, untried?

No, no, we cry, for clearly do we see
that in that song of pageantry and sound
lie all the treasures of a life well lived.
And who'd re-bury treasure once 'tis found?

The riches of your life we all have known,
your children and your husband and your friends;
and who could buy the labor for your own
put forth to keep us clean, and clothed and fed?

And care, that priceless gift when fevers burn,
or weariness or loneliness have reign,
has come from you to each of us in turn.
And would the grass give back the sky its rain?

We cannot give you back your youthful days,
for if we did we'd lose our treasure cave.
Though miracles will come to one who prays,
we cannot ask to lose the gifts you gave.

March 29, 1965

A letter to our daughter, Jo Ann Harris, on our twenty-fifth wedding anniversary

                                        Anchorage, Alaska
                                        March 29, 1965

Silver Threads

Dear Jo,
My baby used to write a rhyme,
    once in awhile.
But now I 'spose you haven't time.
    It's not in style.
Or else the rush of social life—
    It could be such—
has stopped creative writing. Still,
    I doubt it much.

I'd rather think you haven't thought.
    Just slipped your mind.
To put a gift like that aside
    is not your kind.
If inspiration is your lack,
    I'll then proceed.
To give you ample reason now,
    and fill that need.

Your Daddy dear has known the joy
    of married life
full quarter century, that's true,
    with just one wife.
If that won't start the rhyming wheels,
    I don't know Jo.
A poem from your pen is done.
    I know it's so.
        Love,
            Dad

One

One daffodil—
May I send you
one daffodil?

It's new,
and fresh,
and beautiful,
and alive.

It's also
old as time;
sprung from roots
older than years.

One marriage—
fresh and new,
and beautiful,
and living;

Sprung from roots
old as time,
older than years.

December 8, 1970

CONFLICT

In these days of extremes, both in conformity and in non-conformity, I feel some attempt should be made to achieve a proper balance between the two. It was with this in mind that I wrote the following brief essay.

Conformity

I have been accused of being a non-conformist.

A non-conformist is one who refuses to conform to the reasonable and accepted norms and formalities of society.

I believe in driving on the right side of the road; I believe in observing speed limits; I believe in maintaining a reasonable quiet in the late hours of the night; I believe in being sober in public and in observing many other reasonable and accepted rules of society but not because everyone else does but rather for the same reason that others do. It is simply more prudent to do these things in this way.

I believe in respecting the authority of those above me whether or not I can respect the person; I believe in carrying out orders of my superiors on authority alone even if he is wrong, if I have first shown respect for his intelligence by pointing out the error I see.

I am, therefore, definitely not a non-conformist.

Neither, however, am I a conformist.

A conformist is one who blindly follows the thinking of others even if that thinking may be wrong or even injurious to the community, the state, or the nation, or to another group within that entity; he will wear uncomfortable, impractical or even unsightly clothes just because it is the fad (the conformist's word is fashion); he will not question the wisdom or even accuracy of his superiors orders or instructions even if his failure to honor the intelligence of his superior by pointing out those errors should result in embarrassment or chagrin for both; in the same way he carries out instructions in manuals even when their error is glaringly obvious. In other words, he places in those above him (whether in society, his church or his job) Godly attributes attributable only to God.

I most certainly am not a conformist.

December 5, 1964

I know a poet is expected to write beautiful words, lifting words, singing words; but he writes what is filling his heart. Sometimes it is filled with the cruel irony of life.

I had gone to work for a world-known tugboat company in Anchorage. I did so thinking or understanding I would be assistant to the dispatcher, radio operator, and occasional harborcraft skipper: all fun, challenge, and romance connected with the sea. When the following expression burst forth, I was on my way home from a day of hard, dirty, depressing labor cleaning up a barge. I was weary to the core, and thoroughly disillusioned.

> Storms of disillusionment sweep down
> upon the unsuspecting soul;
> the hopeful find their hopes are dashed
> upon the rocky and unyielding shores of life.
> Oh fickle dreams; oh wishes that are but a froth veneer;
> oh when will man perceive
> the hard reality of life and see
> there is no blessing in this life
> but toil.

April 20, 1966

The "News" about My Lai

I cry, I cry for you
who do not understand My Lai.
You are not moaning
for the dead who should have lived.

Of course atrocity could be performed
by one American or ten;
and I say could, not was.
But if it was,
does this make foreign aid by billions
all for naught;
does this make Dr. Dooley and his staff
a bloody group of butchers,
or the Peace Corp Volunteers
"the sons of Capitalistic pigs"?

For if it does,
then this makes every one of us,
including you, my pink-clothed friend,
a worthless clod of earth, not even clay;
for who stands free of sin?

To you who'd drench your land in guilt
and write off all her credits
and her countless deeds of mercy,
all her good
because of this one entry on the debit side;
to you I say, I shudder
for the fire waiting to consume you
in the hungry flames of hell.

You stand here in this free and noble land,
receive her gifts, unearned,

and then, because your guilt becomes a load
you can no longer bear, you try to dump it
on the land that gave you birth.

Atrocity is news, you say.
Then go to where the news is ordered—
Moscow, Peking, or Hanoi—but here,
cast not your stone.
December 11, 1969

SEARCHING

This cry burst forth during my long struggle against, "the call of the sea," and for, remaining with my secure and well paid job as Air Traffic Control Specialist with the Federal Aviation Agency. I am still glad that I answered that call, and, as my beloved son said, "returned to the waters."

Landbound Lament

The sea, the sea, the endless sea
sends out its siren call for me.
Yet oh that call, that haunting call
cannot be heard by one and all,

But only by the hearts attuned
to sense the mysteries it holds,
to feel its healing for my wound,
to hear the challenge to the bold.

A challenge that is not a dare,
but rather invitation there
to see your soul stand tall and free
while held with awe of the endless sea.

March 2, 1964

The End?

Ah, so 'tis happiness you seek, my friend;
is that your goal?
Take care, lest on its placid sea
you strike a shoal
that pinions you and holds you fast,
so that for you there is no future,
only past.

And all the stormy seas that make a man
must crash and roar against some distant shore
where spirits, charged with battle for this life,
see in the storm the chance to say, "I can,
and ask for more."

Ah yes, I sought for happiness, like you;
and I have found it, largely, that is true.
Nor would I change it at this date I guess.
and yet I wonder, could I honestly confess?

Could I speak out in words that do not lie
and say I've missed the opportunity to cry
alone and frightened on that distant shore
where all my passions from my pen could pour
ten thousand words all whetted to an edge
that cut away the numbing fat of peace
and split the soul from bondage with their wedge?

The Lord of Heaven said, "You seek, you find,"
but here, you see, the problem is the kind
of seeking that obsesses one.
For lest you dare, and I mean dare, my friend,
then happiness could truly be
your end.

June 17, 1964

This was written just a few months before I threw prudence, caution, and security to the very winds and left FAA to become a Protection/Boat Officer for the Alaska Department of Fish and Game operating a patrol boat over the vast and endless reaches of Prince William Sound. Did I follow my own advice? Well, some of the poems and essays that follow this one may partially answer that question.

All over Prince William Sound, up the vast fiords and into tiny coves, one is struck with the impossible, yet insistent fact that you are cruising at sea level among the mountaintops. This joining of two extremes, each powerfully impressive in itself, brought forth this poem, written, or more correctly discovered, at sea under a brilliant northern sun:

Prince William Sound, Alaska

Out in the middle of a Switzerland sea
I gaze at the mountains and then look at me.
There's an ocean around me that drops off and away
as the curve of this globe commands it to stay
in the arc that was ordered when molten earth formed
and clouds of the ether thundered and stormed.

I look at myself and I say, "Speck of dust,
by what right do you enter; what is your badge of trust?"
And a Voice from inside me speaks with power so strong
that those mountains have
trembled and made froth of the sea
when that Great Voice just whispered;
and that Voice says to me,

"I command you to enter. I am your Badge of Trust.
For what are the mountains of this Switzerland sea,
what can all this be worth e'en to One such as Me
without man My creation to gaze and behold
and be stirred by the beauty I formed from of old?"

So humbly I enter wearing my Badge of Trust
and thrill to these mountains who now tell me I must
look far and beyond their great towering might
to the Source of all beauty, all power, and light.

Off Port Gravina fiord
Prince William Sound
August 4, 1965

A Sailor's Two Loves

There is a sweet and gently painful loneliness on the sea, somewhat akin to nostalgia, and although on this trip aboard the M/V Brant it was generally well suppressed by the company of two biologists, both lively and friendly extroverts, these men would sometimes leave the ship for half a day at a time, and the full awareness of the sailor's loneliness would have the free course to come to the surface and be known.

And thus it was one long Alaskan afternoon, in the heart of this mountain-torn sea, as I sat down in the silence, alone, to write a letter in:

>Anderson Bay
>Hinchinbrook Island
>Prince William Sound
>Alaska
>August 29, 1965

My beloved family,

The thunder of silence is almost deafening and would be so were it not for the occasional dampening effect of the sound of a raven's call or the cry of a gull or the patter of rain drops on the deck or the rush of an almost imperceptible ground swell on a low gravel bar.

Why is it we find it so necessary, so often, to disturb that perfect harmony of all sound, the silence, with artificial sounds of our own which at best are but distortions of the silence?

Only when we stand in the silence, alone, can we be really aware of standing at the meeting place of two eternities, the past and the future, and look at the mountains as they were in the long past and will be in the distant future but mostly as they are, here, now, in the only reality, the thundering, powerfully eternal and silent present.

And suddenly I am aware that I miss my family; that the magnetic bond that ties a family together has been pulling its slight but persistent, elastic yet indestructible strand; and the burden, like a pail of water carried in the hand, becomes increasingly heavy to bear the longer it is borne.

Yet through the mist that shrouds but never completely hides the future I see myself in the warmth and glow and joy of my family; and I hear another sound, the voice of a siren, the call of the sea; and I know I will have to leave that love for another even before I have returned to my own.

And so it is with those who love the sea: cursed, or blessed (Who is to say?) with two loves, where the wonder of each is somehow magnified by possession of the other; and the sailor finds himself with one plea: love him and let him love you. His love is sweeter, greater, more to be cherished for his other love; and he needs the silence and distance of the sea wherein that love can grow and expand and show itself to him in purity and in power.

Love,
Dad Nichols
Capt., M/V Brant

Our Own

The fog hangs low and drifting, drifting swiftly on the breeze;
the sky peeks through and spreads its blue for a moment on the sea.
The wavelets ring their tinkling bells against the hull;
and from the sky comes the hungry cry of a lonely, gliding gull.

* * * *

Two pursers hang on slanting scopes of anchor line.
The cluster of small boats attached speaks well of wine,
but friendship too and sharing of tall tales
of bigger hauls and thicker fogs and gales.

* * * *

The flooding tide so soon will hide the sand surrounding us,
and then will be but a tiny sea with a wall of mist, and thus
three tiny ships will find themselves at anchor and all alone,
in a world that I, with the mist and the sky and solitude, call our own.

Aboard the M/V Brant
Kanak Island, Alaska
September 9, 1965

Bering River

Following are excerpts from my journal for a period when, as skipper of the Patrol Boat, Brant, for the Alaska Department of Fish and Game, I was sent down to the lonely Bering River area seventy-five miles east of Cordova, Alaska, to police the harvesting of the last salmon run of the year.

Tuesday, Sept. 7, 1965 . . . So interesting what the night tells us and shows us that we cannot see in the daytime for all the light. In the day there are just a number of boats, large and small, anchored here, but at night we live in a city, quite mobile and fleeting to be sure, but still a city: the sounds of engines and voices and radios, traffic busying to and fro, lights marking well each abode, and occasionally the smells of fuel or exhaust, and all punctuated by the stillness and darkness and dampness of the night.

Wednesday, Sept. 8–10 P.M. and I try to review the day. Practically no wind all day, and in the stillness tonight, the distant surf has a soothing sound as does the occasional, almost tinkling slap of tiny wavelets against the hull, or the flicker of flame in the oil pot on the stove. Up at 7:00 for breakfast and then pulled out for the east side for a *much* easier crossing of the bar. Tied to the tender, Blue Bird, for an hour talking to fishermen and watching fish transfer. Word out that the season has been extended for another weekly period of sixty hours starting next Monday at 6:00 A.M., so another week away from home. What paradoxes we humans are, seeking, seeking, seeking for peace, joy, and the vibrant vitality of life in ourselves and our immediate surroundings, and almost, but never quite, finding our treasure. I wouldn't trade my present job for any that I presently know of, and yet often it fails to produce, or perhaps more correctly I fail to find, the romance that any dreamer of a life on the sea should correctly expect. "I am the way, the truth, and the life . . ." and peace, and joy. Why do we so obstinately seek another way?

Thursday, Sept. 9–Most people do "something" wastefully

far too often, because they cannot or will not believe that they can do "nothing" constructively or with profit. The corn grows most while the farmer is doing nothing about it. True, he must plant, cultivate and harvest it (as with man) but it *grows* while he does nothing. Is that not also the same with man? We must practice doing nothing for sufficient periods between the planting and the harvest, else there may be too little to harvest when the time is come. . . .

Saturday, Sept. 11 . . . I guess I need other people more than I realized because I was alone (no visiting) all day yesterday, and by this morning was getting low and blue and wondering what I was really doing out here alone and away from my family; but tonight (after spending half a day exploring the beach with some fishermen), though I still miss my family, there is a fullness and richness to life. Balance is the thing. For each to find (and keep) the proper balance for himself between gregariousness and solitude. Too much of either means too little of the other and like any extreme is an imbalance and thus an eventually intolerable condition.

Wednesday, Sept. 15 . . . Anchored more in amongst the fleet this time so I wouldn't go aground. This anchorage is so tiny that with about twelve pursers and thirty to forty cabin skiffs, we all must anchor much closer than what would be considered good practice in a roomier place. There is one cluster of two pursers and three skiffs fifty feet off my port stern and a cluster of seven or eight cabin skiffs seventy-five feet off my port bow. At low tide this little slot in the sand can't be much over one hundred fifty feet wide and fifteen to eighteen hundred feet long. What is that keen excitement that subtly stirs us when lying at anchor in a good anchorage on a dark night with the rain beating vainly on the roof and the wind roaring its futile defiance through the trees up on the hill? True, the storms in their turn rule us and often bring fear almost to our lips; but now we have the storm walled out, and we revel in the security of our fortress.

Thursday, Sept. 16—I'm tired, and I want to go home. So much in the night that could and should inspire to poetry of thought and expression if not an outright poem: the stillness of motionless air and dry though cloudy skies; the intense darkness jeweled by the lights of this miniature floating city; the silence that is heard as a separate and distinct roar from the incessant roar of the ocean that in itself neither sounds angry nor soothing but weary as one who has fought a losing fight but cannot yet concede defeat even though the sand remains and will yet remain for ages to come. It takes a vibrantly alive mind, not so much to feel and be aware of the poetry of a night (the weariest soul, not asleep, can hear and love a symphony) but to put it into words that record it for others to hear and feel. I weary too easily. I know I'm no more a youth; but by the grace of God I'm a long way from being an old man . . .

Sunday, Sept. 19—Ah, little anchorage, what friendship we have formed so soon. Tomorrow I must hie to the open sea and leave your snug and protective arms. Oh yes, I want to go home, and your pleading and your promises will not detain me; but I shall miss you, little anchorage. The season should end tomorrow, and our little company, our town, our family of common interest will be no more; but tonight, with the rain and the hint of winter in the air, the rows of squared and lighted windows on the pursers strung out behind me speak of coffee and good talk of the season past and talk of plans for the coming winter. Little thought and less talk will there be in those warm cabins of any anticipation of nostalgia concerning you, but I shall not forget. As the ebbing tide holds every boat pointed in the same direction, so does the ending season point us all in one common direction, home; but beyond that our courses will be as variant as the points on a compass, and only I shall remember you and your kindness to us all.

Cordova, Mon. Sept. 20 1965—Death came near today. Hwan Pranto drowned in the breakers trying to come from Bering River, and, although I knew him but one day, I feel as though I have lost someone very close; and there is that subtle searching in the deeper recesses of our minds for clues that we might have said or done something, just a little bit different, and altered, just enough, this tragic course of events. That inscrutable Filipino, who looked the Chinese of his mother, who was a U.S. citizen and knew he must so remain, but who carried the burden of an unfulfillable longing to go back to his own people and help them rise from the slavery of political and religious corruption; this highly educated man who, with his broad mind, was able to talk freely of the true problems of racial prejudice, and yet who showed the weariness and strain of carrying the burden of truth and justice and love in the face of that prejudice; who carried with him the mental material gathered through his years of study and observation for two books on Communism that would not only have helped his people, but all who see hope in Communism, to see that evil for what it is; this simple fisherman who was not simple; this lovely man is now with the Christ whom he loved, and we have lost, for this short time on earth, a brother . . .

Far from being all romance and adventure, life at sea on a small boat can mean long, long hours of weary toil and empty, yet full in their peculiar way, day upon day of infinite loneliness. Yet I find that the weariness is proof for that inner need to know that I have earned my pay; and the loneliness becomes the glass through which I see my life; the frame for the picture of my life; the necessary backdrop for the drama of my life; the illumination for the way of my life.

Because I Must

I'm alone on my ship as the salt sprays fly
and the scattered clouds grace a clear, blue sky;
and a lonely eagle shares my cry,
as he rules his winged throne on high,
that this we know we must do or die.

I'll never know if the tireless sea
can be as lonely for him as it can for me,
or if weary hours dragging endlessly
or if aching bones or back can be
the price he knows he pays to be free.

But I know the price when a long, long run
has kept us going from sun to sun
and my limbs grow weary 'ere the harbor's won;
and I feel all the loneliness of one
who knows he must sail till his life is done.

The blessing of life is toil, they say;
and my worn frame tells that I surely pay.
But the lonely hours are the searching ray
that frames my life; that lights the way;
and I know why I sail on the sea this day.

November 30, 1965

*But the winds of fate blew down my course
and held me to the land.*

Turn Again

Is this why I must turn again
and seek another way;
is this why the waters of my life
are torn and darkened by the tide rips
of a landbound sea;
is it because I love the ocean's endless vastness
whereon the soul of man stands tall and free,
yet find myself by habit bound
within the shelter of the mountain's lee?

It used to be that even here
within the mountain's fold,
the fingers of the sea
reached, green and bold;
and I could reach my hand
and touch the sea
and know, with just a step or two
I could be free.

But through the years the mountains of my life
were washed and worn by storm and time;
and silt has built the bars and shoals
that block the free and living motion of the sea.

Where once the fingers of the sea
reached, green and bold,
a tidal bore now rips the sand
and darkens what were once the living waters

of my hope, the friendly waters,
fresh, inviting to my hand.

I read these lines and see a song
of weary hopelessness,
a resignation more defeat than victory;
and so I turn again and seek another way
because I must, because I must
be free.

March 4, 1970

It was twenty degrees above zero this morning; there were two inches of fresh snow on the ground with the snowstorm continuing through the day. And down in Turn-again-arm, which was, just yesterday in geologic time, a deep, green fiord, the icebergs lie in the mud like huge, black stones; the spring tides roll them over and churn the water and silt into a dark, gray mass.

LLOYD

 Almost two years, two years after our son sailed out across that gulf that separates our fragile, earthly lives from the house of God, I was overwhelmed with the question:

Why?

Why did You take our son?
Did You need him more than we?
Did he do something wrong that You punished him?
Was his role in life ended, finished, completed?
Or had he literally taken a dead-end road?

Why did You take our son?
Did You need him more than we?
Did You not know we needed him?
Or are You saying now that he will do more for us in death
than he could have done in life?
Do You not say, "Love is the essence of the universe"?
Was he not the very essence of love?
Do You say, removing his love from life,
filling our hearts with emptiness, our eyes with tears,
our minds with doubts and confusions,
do You say this is showing us, giving us
love that he could not?

Why did You take our son?
What evil could he have done
that needed to be paid for with his death?
Was it the sin of loving life, of thrilling to its beauty,
of singing its song with voice that brought us all

close to Thy throne;
was it the sin of laughter, of exuberance,
of enthusiasm, of generosity?
Was it the sin of living this earthly life
with a fullness that inspired us all?
Was this his sin?

Why did You take our son?
Did this ending of his life mark its completion?
Was his life completed, at twenty-four?
Were there no more years of his guileless love
left to give to a love-starved world?
Had his almost infinite capacity to love and be loved
reached the finite, at twenty-four?
Was his development finished,
or had it barely begun?
Was the promise we saw
only an illusion?

Why did You take our son?
If he had taken a dead-end road,
was there no turning back or to one side?
Did he not know he was on such a road?
Did he never ask Thee for guidance?
Do You ask us to believe
he was insensitive to Thy direction?
Could You not have stopped him
and then set him on a new course?
Was there no way
but to stop him dead?

Why did You take our son?
Could we have him back any other way
but without this knowledge of his death?
Could we have him back any other way
but on the road he was traveling?

Could we have him back any other way
but bound, immersed, drowning
in the sea of conflict within him?

We know why You took our son, oh God, we know,
but oh the pain, the pain,
the awful, hurting emptiness
where once we held our son.

October 25, 1968

It is almost amusing, even in the face of such irony, that such bitterness could have come out of such a beautiful person.

The Rape of Mind

The ugliness of knowledge rapes my mind of the goodness in man. How vile and base are we that feign such pious virtues. How dare we deliberately proclaim ourselves in the image of God? Does our questionable possession of an open mind, the "live and let live" make us free from ourselves? No! we must hide somewhere as we fail to be the very thing we profess.

Like winter's violence to a budding willow, the plague of knowledge took me. How I fought the chill; but still, I feel the guilt as I meet myself in others. Yes, we are but in the likeness of evil.

Sometime between 1963 and 1965
Lloyd Nichols

The River

How does one stop a river? Remove the sun, so that no vapors rise from restless seas? Or stop the wind and tell it, "Carry not your moisture-laden clouds against my mountains." Or tell the rugged peaks not to pierce the gentle clouds and make them cry? How does one stop the rain from falling? Unless we do, those countless tears of heaven will gather in the crags and forests, become a stream, a waterfall, a creek and then, a river. And there it is, a flowing river.

Many years ago a group of men looked at a river, the mighty Columbia, and said, "We'll stop it here. We'll build a dam of concrete, rock and steel." They named the dam to be, The Dalles, the Celilo Indian name for "falling waters," because the lake to form would cover up forever, those tumbling, rushing, restless waters where Indians for centuries had caught the sea-grown salmon in the spring and fall.

The men hired engineers; the best of science set to work to think. Core drills were put to work, and samples of the soil and rock below were drawn from deep inside the earth. The dam took shape on countless sheets of paper. The minds of men envisioned every ton of steel, every sack of cement, every grain of sand that would be needed to form the massive barrier that would stop a river.

And then for three years it looked as though confusion ruled the desert and the river there. Tugboats pushed drill rigs, barges and bucket dredges up and down; dynamite exploded with thunder heard for miles, and timbers, rock and water were hurled high up into the sky; the debris seemed to be suspended there as if, like a ballet dancer, the broken pieces were reluctant to return to earth.

But steadily the bed took shape, as the brilliant engineers had planned. Steel, tons of it, was tied in place; from thousands of board feet of lumber, forms were built, and into them countless (no, not countless, for the engineers had counted even every grain of sand) tons of concrete were poured.

One day the dam was finished. The gates were open, and the river rushed through, as it had been doing for centuries before man was able even to conceive of stopping a river. A crowd was gathered; loudspeakers were set up, and a man, a tiny drop of living matter, almost unseen there before the dam spread out across the mighty river, spoke into a microphone; and he said, "Friends, we are gathered here as witness to a great event in the progress of man. In a few moments, a member of the cabinet of the President of the United States, the greatest power on earth, will press a button, and the gates will close. He will, with the pressing of a single button, stop a river, the mighty Columbia. I know, when this happens, you will share with me a powerful emotion; chests will feel constricted, tears will well up in eyes and roll quietly down cheeks, for at that moment we will be witnessing the culmination of an achievement of science and of man's mind that few in history will have shared. For all of us really share in this achievement, all of us are really pressing that button, all of us are really stopping a river. But share with me now, one question, 'For how long?' We shall alter, slightly, the form of the river for a few miles; the lake we build will cover the old 'falling waters,' and The Dalles will now produce electric power for us. But friends, fellow workmen, engineers, scientists, we cannot stop a river."

The Honorable Secretary of the Interior stepped forward and pressed the button, and massive gates began to close. And as the waters rose behind the dam, one could see that in so little a while the gates would have to be partially reopened, or the river would rise, seek its way around or over the dam and continue its endless and irrepressible giving of itself to the sea.

How does one stop a love that shows itself as grief? Remove the sun of his smiles, the memory of his eyes, his warmth, his radiant presence, so that no vapors rise from the restless seas within us? Or stop the wind of our emotions and tell it, "Carry not your moisture-laden clouds against the mountains that he left within us, his strength, his convictions, his fine mind, his warmth and responsiveness and loveliness."? Or tell those stalwart peaks not to pierce the gentle clouds and make them cry? How does one stop the rain of love from falling? Unless one does, those countless tears of heaven will gather in the crags and forests, and become a stream, a waterfall, a creek, and then a river. And there it is, a flowing river of love.

And even if that river shows itself as grief, who can stop it, or would even try?

March 24, 1968

I would rather write words of joy, but sadness and darkness are part of life too; so we must keep something of a balance, or we might lose even the guideline of the "straight and narrow" entirely from our sight.

These are words of sadness.

My Son's Birthday

The tears could flow as easily today as yesterday; for what is really more, twenty-eight years, or twenty-eight years and a day? He's gone, and the empty void he left is too large, *too* empty to be filled.

World problems, family problems, personal problems, all had a way of falling into a simpler and thus truer perspective when shared with him. We need his trust, his faith, his love that amplified our qualities because he did not see or acknowledge our faults.

We need him, we need him;
                      and the tears can do no more than show how hopeless
                is our missing him.

March 25, 1970

An Unapprehended Inspiration

A poem,
    fragile as a candle's flame,
                begins;
A cold breeze snuffs its life away.

A crystal wonder called a snowflake forms
and starts its journey to the ground;
it melts before it settles to the earth
and falls instead

    only as a wet drop
              of cold rain
                        upon my face.

A river starts
high in some Australian mountain
and falls with free abandon
to the desert floor;
the heat and sand evaporate
and drink its life away,
so that it never knows the sea.

And even this same sea
has swept away a life
that had so much to give,
and this
              on the eve of its promise
                          of fulfillment.

We speak of the cycle of life;
but that cycle implies fulfillment
within its cycle.
What of those
who never reach fulfillment;
what of them?

Mankind must know
the crystal wonder always new,
as well the sea would die
if rivers never reached its shores.
And he must be renewed with youth,
or old men tottering to their graves
would have no one to leave their wisdom to.

But most of all
the flame of inspiration

must be protected,
    nourished,
        loved,
not snuffed out;
for without inspiration
     all life is meaningless
and less
    than a vanishing river

or a melted snowflake.

March 28, 1970

After my son left, more than a year passed before I was able to write anything about him; and even then, although it came from deep inside, it had a bitter tone. I guess I was angry with God, and told him so. This is more truly what he was:

The Light That Cannot Die

We thought, perhaps,
as months passed slowly into years,
we thought our pain of grief,
that awful hurting emptiness,
would fade away,
and we would then be free.

But can we ever free ourselves
of that to which we cling
with every fibre of our hearts,
with every sinew of our souls?

This little speck of dust we call the earth
has circled twice around her mother sun;
the frozen ground we opened for his grave
has thawed and frozen, thawed and frozen now again,
since he, intending only one short sail
across Alaska's Gulf,
sailed on, instead, across that gulf
that separates our frightened, earthly shells
from his eternal home.

The light we called our son,
the light that drew its power from
a source that only God can know,
the light we saw expressed
as joy of life, enthusiasm, ebullience, and love,

that light is that same light
that must not fade, that will not die.

Wih every fibre of our hearts,
with every sinew of our souls we cling;
for in this world of darkness, hate, and greed,
we see the double, vital need
to pour out love and have that love received.

Like rain poured out upon the earth,
we wish to see our love absorbed,
and from the joining of this rain and earth,
to see things grow.
How could life be
if earth turned back the rain?

His very life was guileless love,
but full and rounded and complete;
his full capacity to love
was balanced by that equal vital need,
for he received our love.

This pain of grief,
this awful hurting emptiness
will never fade away;
but as the months pass slowly into years,
we see those tears turn slowly into steel,
the cables bonding to our hearts
this light that can not die.

November 25, 1968

BEAUTY AND LOVE

My Cabin Door

A simple wooden door, made out of spruce in fact,
and I can here assure you it is more than tacked.
For it is nailed one thousand times it seems.
The night 'twas done I nailed them all again in dreams.

The outside boards from local trees were sawn,
their color creamy tan; well, like a fawn.
The grain is course and rough. No Sitka spruce were these.
Susitna Valley land produced these trees.

The layer next is set at forty-five degrees
to give it strength and warmth more than to please.
But still, it pleases me. I know each piece that's there;
for that's the story here: of love and care.

The inside layer is a joy to gaze upon.
From Sitka spruce these lovely pieces sawn.
Fine textured is the artist's word for such a wood.
I matched them up together best I could.

The handles are a piece of sturdy one by four.
No question here whereon to grasp the door.
And in their strength a comfort deep is felt and known;
secure and warm e'en when I'm here alone.

But oh those hinges, massive, black and rusty things;
I wouldn't trade them for the golden ones of Kings.

Scrounged from abandoned mine or some mysterious
 place
they add the perfect final touch upon the face

Of this, my simple, lovely, wooden cabin door;
but then I've told you all of this before.
But what I haven't said and what is really there
is evidence of work and love and care.

June 30, 1966

Love

No one has ever fully defined love and, fortunately for mankind, no one ever will; for like life it is an infinite thing reaching even beyond the stars.

The human mind, too, is an infinite thing, and without love and life and the stars there would be no wondrously infinite challenge to the mind.

But there are limited (and beautiful even within their limits) definitions of love that give us stepping stones across the endless ocean of understanding and, if taken with care and patience and wonder, these stepping stones can become islands of beauty and joy.

One of these islands is the definition of love as, "The intense awareness of another person," and, I might add, of a place, a sport, a job, a field of flowers or a single leaf, the sweet and peaceful loneliness of the wilderness, of life.

How seldom have we listened so carefully to the sound of the breeze that we could hear it caress each single leaf on the trees embracing us?

How seldom have we listened so intensely to the silence that we were aware of its roar even above the sound of a city; or if alone in the wilderness, have we been grateful for the dampening effect of the song of a bird or the sigh of the wind or the buzzing of a fly in the window lest the roar of the silence be deafening to our untrained ears?

We have ridden on boats and failed to realize love for this incredibly variable experience, because we failed to observe with careful attention the lovely curve of the bow wave or the symmetrical pattern of the wake as the waters, patiently and without anger, returned to their tranquillity.

There are many passing experiences with this definition of love, and we recognize them: the squish of sand between our toes on an ocean beach, the mystically subtle excitement of the smell of damp and freshly turned earth, the beauty of a sunset or sunrise when we took the time to count the infinite pattern of color as it told its mystic story to us.

These are but feeble examples. We all could make our endless list of those moments when we knew love in this limited but very real sense; and we must confess, as we mentally jot them down, that we must include people as well as places and things.

So engrossed with our "goal" in life (few indeed could define theirs and they often in error) we blunderingly crash along and miss the only goal we can reach, the here and now when we can love, when we can be intensely aware of the life around us.

It cannot come easily, this ability to love; for, like the pearl of great price, it must be bought; and the purchasing medium is effort and practice and failure and effort and practice again.

But this goal of goals like the love that it is is worth infinitely more than we are asked to pay; for when we can learn to love we can "have life and have it more abundantly."

June 30, 1966

The Manliness of Beauty

Men have often thought, in their blind error, that poetry was sissy stuff. That men who fashion words into a song or catch the lovely scented flower or eerie light of evening's afterglow into a worded frame and paint thereon the beauty that they see, they thought, with even some contempt, that these were women in disguise. For surely men in all their virile strength would not descend to stirrings of the inner self.

But oh the error of these children thought as men. For beauty is the gift of God who through his son the Christ proved manhood in a thousand ways beyond the blunt, crude measure of brute strength.

For God has chosen man to re-create and yet create again the beauty of this world of ours. Observe the bridge across the way. The beauty of its arch is there as long as it will stand. And ships at sea; such loveliness is from the hand of men and steered by men they swing their perfect arcs across the sea.

Oh women have their place in beauty's scheme; and I would

not belittle all they've done to lift the soul of man, but 'tis man's world and woman for him made; and if at times she lifts the pen to tell the beauty of the life she sees, she is not using tools belonging solely to her own but using tools of men to point the men again to beauty's way.

The beauty of a child in Mother's arms; oh all the world agrees the fairest picture of them all; and yet it must be known, man plants the seed and from that seed the beauty of a child is born.

Oh think not men that scoffing at the poet's hand as feminine and weak and small makes you the greater man of all.

No more than God's great gift of beauty to a girl makes her a woman true does God's great gift of virile strength make you a man. It's what we do with those born talents that we have that mold us into men or women true; and though taming of the world is man's primary task, he cannot tame the world and never ask, "Why do I do this thing but to release the beauties of her treasures fair and thus discover life with all its lovely depth and purpose and its truth."

July 2, 1966

Anchorage, Alaska
September 16, 1964

Dearest Jo,

    Forty-five years and some days ago, my Mother brought forth upon this continent a new son; conceived in love and dedicated to the proposition that perhaps he might contribute some small measure to the betterment of this vain and sordid earth while at the same time finding those necessary odd moments of peace and rest, and also of gaiety, and even indulgence.

    Just how much he has or will have contributed to that betterment only history can tell, if indeed history will be able to find record of him in the maze of ordinary people; but I can report that he has found many of those necessary "odd moments" and is at this moment (1:00 A.M., Sept. 16, 1964) experiencing one of peace, rest, and indulgence.

My Tankard

I thank you Jo for such a precious gift,
an old gray mug of lead and stuff, and tin,
cast in the sand that left its mark within
where now the bitter ale rests cold and clear.

A tankard of such style graces beer
with all the comradeship of other years.
It brings in proper focus once again
the true relationship of "now" and "then."

Without a "then" our "now" has no foundation;
(Without a history how can we guide our nation?)
No look back down the trail now and then
will mean we'll make the same mistakes again;

And worse, forget the peace and comradeship
an old gray mug of lead and tin can bring

when chilled and filled right to its foaming top
with brew as old as yeast and grain and hop.

So thank you Jo for such a precious gift.
It really gave your Daddy quite a lift.

With love,
Daddy

Many years ago, when my first love was flying, a poem started deep inside of me. One day, when the wings lifted me into the endless, blue sky, a song burst forth:

> Ah, such winged things we fly
> up in this wild and yonder
> everlasting sky.

The months and years passed; I came to Alaska, joined a flying club, and the northern skies amplified the song and added the words:

> Yes, poets write and angels sing,
> but could it ever be that Kings
> could ask for more than wings?

One day, perhaps eight or ten years after the first words of the song became a part of my flying experience, the song asked for completion; and the last two verses came into being:

> For aeroplanes are not machines
> of soulless wood and steel
> and other things,
> but are themselves alive and free
> yet giving of that life to me.

> For who could ride upon the winds
> on wings in endless sky,
> and not believe those wings were part
> of God's eternal why.

April 1968

Some people like to pick berries; I like to pick words (they grow everywhere) and gather them, and press them and maybe add some sugar of love and yeast of life, and brew them, and bottle them, and age them, just to see what kind of wine I can produce. Here, try a glass of this:

Gray

Is gray a color?
Gray is really colorless, isn't it?
Astronaut Lovell said, "The moon is colorless,
like grayish, deep sand."

I look out my office window and see the gray fog;
no life, no action, no color.
Gray clouds take the color from the sky.
A gray dawn means a colorless sunrise.

I remember my father's obsidian-black Indian hair
losing its color and turning gray.
I remember a lovely old nurse whose glorious hair
lost its golden glow and turned to gray.
I remember the colorless, gray face of grief.

But if gray is not a color, then what is gray?
Gray is the gathering of color, like the silence
that is the perfect harmony of all sound.

Sand: the gathering of countless particles of rock
of every hue; look at one of these wonders
under a microcope.

Fog: the diffusing of color;

every color of the magnificent spectrum is there;
through the gentle mist flows action and life.

Hair: rich and full and colorful lives are proven
by this gathering of the sands of time;
noble gray hair.

Grief: only they who can know the color of love,
the intense, blazing color of love,
only they who have seen that color ground to bits of sand
can know the noble gray of grief.

Noble gray.
All pervading gray.
Is God gray?

January 24, 1969

The creation of this poem was sparked by an abstract painting by my daughter, Judy Holtmann. For the painting spreads out before our eyes, the universal struggle between the call of the glory of God, and the fascinating, sometimes irresistible temptation of the lower flames, bending and burning our weak and mothlike wings. When beauty envelops us, who is to say from whence its source?

A Splash of Color
(Ordered by Celestial Law)

Is this a sunrise
caught in that brief hour
when the flame of day begins?

Is this a sunset
where the gathered coals of burning day
are banked in glory here
before the sleep of night?

Or is this Hell's inferno
searing 'cross the soul of man?

The love of woman, God,
what beauty tearing at his heart,

and oh, what hell.

For he who loves
sees color in the drabbest dawn
and knows a sunset rare
though clouds and rain obscure
the fall of night.

But he who loves can also know
the dark, bewitching beauty
of the flames of hell
and find his flame of joy
is but a part of Hell's inferno,
searing 'cross the soul of man.

November 21, 1969

To a Mother, a Grandmother, and Three Daughters

Re: Arrangement of five roses.
October 9, 1967
Orders to my florist

Dear Sir:

This must be a very special arrangement. It will require the touch of a master, the sensitiveness of one who deeply loves and understands flowers; this must be arranged with real love.

I shall leave the selection of a vase to you; but I do have this to say, it must be a lovely vase, yet not too lovely, for it must support the flowers, enhance their beauty, yet take nothing from them. These are very, very special roses; and each holds its own unique and very special position in this bouquet.

Just the right distance above the vase, there must be two pink rosebuds side by side. They must be a strong pink however; nothing pale or weak will do. They must be buds, showing that glorious promise that rosebuds do; but each can have two or three petals just starting to unfold. Choose their size and color carefully, for they must show that youthful vitality that is the very life of life.

Highest and to the left, place a large, deep red rose. One of those that have aged enough to have turned almost a dark lavender near the center, spreading to that soft, yet strong, deep red toward the edges that older roses do—a color that implies a strength and wisdom with its beauty and gentle fragrance. As I said, this must not be a young rose, but take care that there are no flaws, no curled edges or torn petals. I expect this rose to be with the bouquet for some time.

A little lower and to the right, place a bright, red rose, one that even you, who look upon flowers all the day, would stop to look upon again. It should not be a rosebud, but neither should it be quite fully blossomed out. The exact stage of development is very critical with this rose, for its beauty, and its depth, and its love of life must be clearly evident, yet, its not-quite-complete development must show an exciting promise.

Now here, your skill as a florist will be truly tested. Yellow is my favorite color, but I am most particular about the correct shading. In the center and a little forward, place a large, yellow rose, absolutely flawless, fully bloomed, yet showing the stamina, vitality and enthusiasm for much life to come. Take care that the shading is soft and tender and kind and understanding, yet bright with the exuberance of life. It must hold itself erect with authority, yet with justice, with strengh, yet with tender love, but above all, it must display a depth of loveliness not found in many roses.

Sincerely,
Dean Nichols

I shan't really order the flowers, for what florist could ever be expected to arrange such a bouquet; but wouldn't it be something if he could?

A letter to my daughter, Jo Ann Harris, about her brother Lloyd's baby, Kimberly June

Anchorage, Alaska
February 15, 1965

Dear Jo,

I thought you ought to know
that Kimmy learned to crawl today.

You see,
the Herculean task of learning for a child
is something that we take for granted;
but we sleep;
for right before our eyes we see Mount Everest won,
and bathyspheres descend the Marianas Deep.

We see man's wondrous find of fire
turn into stoves and ships and planes
and rockets higher.

The budding mind that first observes,
then questions, then desires,
has found itself on one side of the room,
as far from toy as birthplace from the tomb.

Yet faint remembered thought that hand will pull

has tumbled next to one that knee will push,
that each hand has its own control,
each knee and toe is separate from the other.

She's found with crashing thunder no less loud
that these things fit together as the cloud
above the Atom Bomb has told the earth
those atoms are but parts of all that's worth.

And so she learned to crawl today.
I thought you ought to know,
dear Jo

                                            **Love,
Dad**

Even the most discriminating connoisseur would not expect to find a perfect wine, for that would end his searching.

He spends his life instead seeking the best, and that only the best for a special occasion, or the best from a certain vine. Always there is the margin for improvement; and that is what makes the difference.

A Glass of Rare Wine
(Vintage 1893)

Who is this youth with the fresh ideas,
the vibrant, exciting view of life?
Who is this person whose sage wisdom
has grown from the years?

Who is this woman who has known a thousand storms,
yet who thrills to a new storm
because it is new?

Who is this child who sees today and tomorrow
as the most exciting days of all,
because only they can hold promise?

Who is she who knows no age
because she knows the timelessness
of beauty and love?

Who is my love who sets me free
from the only chains that can bind me,
those I place upon myself;
who is she who sets me free
just by her love?

Who is this glass of rare wine,
filled to its sparkling edge
    with fresh, vibrant youth tempered with years,

  with the challenge of a storm yet with the daring
to thrill and laugh in the face of the storm;
  with the promise of tomorrow built
on the wonder of today;
  with the intensity of now amplified
by the timelessness of time;
  with freedom from the only jailer, self;
who is she?

Well let me say, to me
she is an aunt, a friend,
a teacher, a student,
a confessor, a confidant,
a guiding rod of iron,
a unique and special creation by the hand of God
made all the more lovable by her possession
of the human frailties that make her of the earth;

Her name is Laura.

December 15, 1969

The Gift

Poetry, elusive gift,
where have you gone?
I see the snow,
and it is only snow,
and white.
Where are the words
refracting countless colors
from the light?

Oh fragile gift,
I know you sleep and are not gone;
I know you will return
as surely as the setting sun
predicts the dawn.

But golden gift,
for having known you
I could cry.
Impatiently I wait
the healing of my soul,
so that your silent power
may speak again,
            and yet again, before
I fade into the night of life
and die.

March 12, 1971

www.ingramcontent.com/pod-product-compliance
Lightning Source LLC
Chambersburg PA
CBHW051701090426
42736CB00013B/2486